Goya's L.A.

Other books by Leslie Scalapino
Considering how exaggerated music is
that they were at the beach — aeolotropic series
way (These North Point titles available from Sun &
Moon Press)
The Return of Painting, The Pearl, & Orion / A Trilogy ,
North Point Press
Crowd and not evening or light, O Books & Sun & Moon
Press
How Phenomena Appear to Unfold, Potes & Poets Press
Defoe, Sun & Moon Press
Objects in the Terrifying Tense / Longing from Taking Place,
Roof Books

Goya's L. A.

Leslie Scalapino

Potes & Poets Press, Elmwood, Connecticut, 1994

Designed by Leslie Scalapino

Acknowledgments

The cast (at the time of writing this) in performance at The Lab in San Francisco (1994) included: Yoshi Akiba as Dead Souls; Zack directed. Larry Ochs composed music for saxophone for the performance.

The image of figures running biting in the crowd was inspired by a passage from Kevin Killian's story 'Biography' which he read at Intersection (1993).

The author also wishes to thank Sue and Bill Elmore for their slides of the rotting coyote landscape; and for the use of their greyhounds which flew for the play in photos taken by Leslie Scalapino and Sue Elmore.

A section from the play was published in *New American Writing*.

The Text as Visual

Author's Introduction

The performance of the play, *Goya's L.A.*, is images occurring in a rhythm of presentation as if 'not planned' as, but are, elements of a linear plot; the structure is therefore 'open' and somewhat camp in tone as if the structure is forgotten (has to be by the audience, because it becomes extended).

"Events take place, singly, at a rhythm that is their simple occurrence." It is their own occurrence, which is loose because these cannot be seen, or occur, in a plot. The events are discrete episodes as if constituting real 'history', therefore slight and depressed as plot. Their 'order' is only seeing them, what they are. Their rhythm of presentation is finding the birth, the place in occurrence we're seeing, of these single scenes and events.

Presentation is visual events spoken, such as the sumo floating on the ocean horizon, being real scrutiny of the vertical and horizontal line, of our vision as per the set itself.

The sense of the vertical ad or billboard space being 'free', non-real fantasy, as being therefore a constructing of seeing, is extended and disrupted, but also created by a visual sense of the horizontal 'places'/ scenes of events occurring in the plot, *as if these are real*.

I want the play to be, to reduce to, one's inner apprehension *as* action.

Techniquely, this means (in terms of the presentation not based on 'ordering', of chronological plot or visual scenes): the 'extreme' conflict in the adolescent, which later may unfold as the serene observation in the adult — these two are not separate, *are* the vertical and horizontal observing themselves. This observation is the actual visual presentation of the play.

The progression of the play, not being based on ordering as plot, is based on statement of its form, *as* the ordering factor.

It cannot be based on plot except as 'unknown' (to the audience) chronology of visual scenes, because action is solely the inner apprehension in a person there.

'Inner occurrence' (as action) takes place somewhere in the play, and at some time then in the audience.

Inner apprehension occurs after, later, in both performance and audience as if from actions. Yet it is somehow first.

For example, Defoe at the play's end 'states' the physical, spatial phenomena of love, which has been brought into existence. It has a spatial location by its inner location as text, spoken, which occurs 'alone', separate from (its) visual images (which are seen, and also apprehended as not real, at the instant they're emerging):

The non-existence of or no ordering by government and Akira's jetting on the dark then ejaculating a black cloud in the night on which he hangs, makes the proximity the vertical and horizontal rim we're seeing.

The sensibility is feminist in listening to an illusory structure of reverberations, where spoken language is not 'realistic' 'representative' and therefore gets at an inner ('outside') sound (neither male nor female, nor

6

class denotated) but which appears as these outside as 'mimic'.

'Camp' is fake transitions, so that a structure (of only change) is visible. She is even being mocked in her own tone, which induces only changes.

Visually, one sees in apparently inner captions. We don't know what writing is.

The tone of *Goya's L.A.* is somewhat comparable with Romance comic books or the recent Chinese film, *The Killers*, which is only action and, like the Romance comics, *stills* of the person seen separate (alone) in an 'immortalized', camp moment, that is, 'captured' from the side, sitting drinking a Scotch, for example; but where the person with whom the conversation is occurring then doesn't appear in the still: as if *that* person, who is only *another* character in the film or Romance comic, is the 'viewer' who later 'remembers' that loved person existing only in the still — a double nostalgia (and as if the heroic moment were in a gesture drinking scotch) — where neither ever existed.

There is only action (continual gun battles, in which killing or being killed doesn't matter) and sentiment. The sentiment in *The Killers* is based on a 'fake' nostalgia for the killer and his male friend (our and their perceiving that) whose 'characters' don't exist; so the observer at any point constantly vanishes.

If sentiment (and) (action, perception of which is sentiment) is the only basis, the structure is entirely transitory.

In *Goya's L.A.*, sentiment (the only standard) is observed from within, where action is the only visible occurrence.

That is seeing the minute motions of the transient inner realm.

The inner realm itself is made transient, in order to see it.

'Goya's seeing' ('in any period') is incidental (incidents, located), which is the only history:

"Just have moves be in tandem. This play induces movement that is minute and has no function, requiring complete attentiveness.

Not having a function is attentiveness. Is joy memory or is it this movement?

The phrases continue to change to become movement in itself. The movement induces a greyhound flying curled legless."

Goya's L.A.

a play by Leslie Scalapino

Characters:

Dead Souls — A Japanese woman. She wears highheels and a slinky dress, occasionally a kimono over it.

Defoe — A woman, sprightly in manner. She wears a slinky dress.

Akira — A man who is Defoe's image of a young boy who is a samurai, though he is a man. Sometimes wears a samurai armour constructed from photo and cardboard; or the suit may hang 'disembodied' in the air on the set. Akira may also double as the **Muscular Dove**, who wears soft white wings on padded shoulders, is handsome with mask of bleached white hair and black brows.

Shadow-Akira — A Japanese man speaking the lines in Japanese.

The Officer — A Black or African-American man or woman who wears a dark blue policeman's uniform. He

9

may double as **Grey Silk Suit Man,** who is gloved, is faceless with ratlike stitched hole for a face (one mask) and with a 'worm face' (second mask of same person seen again) with billowing windblown suit.

The Muscular Dove and Grey Silk Suit Man — May be played by separate actors, rather than by Akira and The Officer, or may be played by the same actor.
Woman #3 — taped voice of a woman

Possibly use of **Voice of Gray Silk Suit Man** taped voice of a man

Set:

A platform in center stage which has a shelf above, attached at the back of the platform. The shelf runs the length of the back of the platform. A cardboard cloud may be on the ceiling which conceals a fetus-doll on a cord.

The action and set uses the imaginative vertical space of ads, but with the 'horizontal' sense of multiple events and scenes that are real, extending, interceding, also disrupting a space that's 'free' fantasy (as advertisement becomes an object *seen* and only by one). While seen en masse, it's as if it is seen by one by its *being* the form of the mass technique.

Act I: Scene 1

Both **Akira & Defoe** wander out into the audience now, **Akira** standing with his hands down and eyes gazing downward in one place and then another (he pulls down a flap on his chest showing gilded rose chest cavity, in samurai armor) while **Defoe** moves speaking with barely suppressed passion (where she is being mocked by her own tone, to which she responds lightly or not at all) wandering in the audience. Behind them is the figure of **Dead Souls** lying illuminated in rose light and wearing a Marilyn Monroe mask.

Defoe: Akira has been wounded. I have him in hiding, lying in the gel of his own chest.

The rose glow of the pearl on its shell, he can't move, lying.

I have to escape what is closing in on me, so I want to write for the newspaper.

Seeing him, not in memory, as occurring somehow, shows *how* it occurs in present time, only.

I walk across a street and tiny black birds flew in rushes around me so that their bellies were to me.

They float by, I'm still. I was in misery. I don't know why.

Vast minute swirls in the air of bellies floating by, on the currents, I walked. There were so many there they fell from the air.

It didn't open. This is a slogan.

No one shot.

Walking is the waves rolling in a bank. People in them are swept in a line.

I didn't have any dreams last night so there's nothing there. That occurs.

The people were in retreat being fired on facing back. That's a decal. It's caused by printing. Itself.

It's the only writing. That's what I want.

That's like saying I worked for a dollar twenty-five cents.

We can't own anything.

That way.

If I don't have the job of a nomad, they eat sugar then. later.

Not being in a building, for work, won't be anything. That's good.

If you have to learn something new every time, one doesn't come to anything. That's our civilization seen as if looking at it through it. One shouldn't begin to learn.

My ideal was to be a soldier.

Walking in a line, but for several months only.

I can only work for a while and not *for* anyone.

The most unusual thing was the fish leaping into our hands because they'd never seen people, from the streams.

That's the only thing I remember, when we were retreating, panning. This is a perversion of it. There isn't memory. Really.

We can really see.

Akira: Though that happened. Then it occurs.

Defoe: The people I respect for their ability and merit don't care about me. At all.

Whether I have ability, which I do as they do. Or am serene. Just not caring about me. That.

Akira (his tone in smiling is neutral, ironic): Say you're valued.

Defoe: I want to get everything I think.

So I may not introduce new things. I'm not valued. This may repeat and go on and on the same. Then I'll see *how* it occurs. I don't know the content. What is it?

Akira (deadpan, neutral, smiling): How are you going to build, to revolt, that?

Defoe: This woman came to the door. She asked me if I had heard of someone, a savior, so I wouldn't know this.

When I say, really wondering, *you mean Jesus?* She says, yes.

How do I live here?

Akira: I see.

Defoe: Writing was changed by war. After. The same writing that was existing then before, became changed. The movement induces a greyhound flying curled legless.

This was discovered by Goya. Behavior goes on, but writing is not existing

Then when new things were written, this was also going on. That it was changed, wasn't existing.

We're not existing.

Not having a function is attentiveness. Is joy memory or is it this movement?

One can't be a writer to do that. I don't find out.

The Long March occurred before that then. As a result.

Akira: (indicating audience) They don't know when it occurred. That's right.

Defoe: Goya observes yet we don't suffer
when we see the day moon existing
but not seeing as a function of memory
Did Goya see without memory?
The tiny black birds rush one

Akira: (as if asking if one is able to talk at all, in general)
Can I talk?
They're rushing by
lying in a hay stack
on the ground

That's a slogan.
That exists
I was depressed
then.

Defoe: Goya made it by depressing it. Then it begins. It has no being.

VO of woman #3: (Akira & Defoe freeze, and then walk and freeze gazing down)
There can't be any movement of people.
They stand at the side.
They never move amidst the hanging slabs, then stand in the audience after a while.
They stand in a group as if in a field, not working, with their hands down.
They're loitering. I saw these men simply standing in fields, when I was driving.
There'd be some.
Then more further on.
They were guards of dope in mountains, though they were standing in fields.
People are standing. Their eyes move. They don't face each other. There.

Defoe: Sometimes one is so depressed it is like heavy water moving on one. One is still.
not coming out for days – from one's apartment –
comes out. walking.
but where it and one *(is)* submerged — it is there. There's no one there. It's where the person is walk-

ing, there's no one there, and there's no feeling or recipient of it. Right then.

That's the only place.

Being clubbed while they are clear inside, out practicing this freely in a disciplined way. That is solely public.

that one should wash the toilet bowl — where patricians are weak — a location is just itself

opens like the moon hanging on the crowd.

Their memory is not a function of the crowd.

Goya didn't see them.

He sees it when it begins.

Being depressed walking occurs before Goya sees.

My being depressed is not related to social behavior. I walked out first.

They don't see me. I see them.

Tie their shoe. One is moving in water. Without dreams. At all.

I was preparing an index, as a job, and I made lots of mistakes.

I stayed up without sleep because I couldn't do this simple job.

Pretending to be a patrician, some other doing so, which is empty, had real ability. (**Akira** exits)

Scene 2

(**Slide** is shown on center wall of rotting coyote landscape with the caption underneath: pretence of a patrician is being) Music: cicadas screaming.

Dead Souls: So this is only memory, and it goes forward.

 With the rotting corpse sapped in the bulb of the
sun falling in the entire blue sky that's floating.

 The hull of the president's helicopter coming in
in the black night, the fish are popping on the surface,
flying. That are people also.

(Another **slide** of rotting coyote landscape collaged with
lotuses. **Shadow-Akira**, to one side as if dreaming,
speaks the following passage in Japanese before Dead
Souls says it.

There's only their flying as the helicopters are coming in wallowing on the burning sheet with the flares coming off of it illuminating the swimmers in it.

V.O. of woman: This is to isolate the shape or empty interior of some events real in time so their 'arbitrary' location to each other emerges to, whatever they are.

Defoe (musing as if watching it, just making it out, looking forward at audience):

The swimmers in the burning fields are larvae popping on it. Larvae singed coming up off of it are illuminated. It's reflecting widely.

Rotting dog that's beautiful reflecting on the bulb of the sun, swimmers are moving to it there.

For the actual Romantics reality was incredible. Here, it is. So history is our form of scrutiny.

Dead Souls: The structure is the relation of occurrences, but it itself is qualitatively different from these.

(turning away, referring to the swimmers): Waist deep *their* soldiers were burning in it.

Bulbous thrashing the bulb is squeezed out of one. I was down on the ground thrashing.

Defoe: As there's only action
Events occur solely.

They're soldiers and so one's heart burst
The hyena is swimming ahead in the indigo water. It is head swimming in the incredibly blue void then.

19

That could be an ad.

Sumo is barely seen floating bulk on the ocean.
Sagging mass floats on the thin surf.
That's a sumo that's on sand. (Music fades)

A sumo and a hyena are the only creatures swimming on the ocean then. They don't make a sound.

Dead Souls (Shadow-Akira exits. Dead Souls speaks to audience, as if to one person): This isn't vision.
This can't be a vision just *as such,* any more, therefore suppressed in the physical state it emerges.

Scene 3

Slide: of a greyhound running. Then darkness. **The officer** walks down center amidst audience while speaking in darkness (series of slides of greyhounds moving away or toward the viewer) moving from the audience down the center aisle to the stage area and onto it. **Akira** comes on stage and speaks in the dark. Music: cicadas in their highpitched screaming. Saxophone.

Officer: The darkness collapses softly on the folded greyhound with no legs floating toward one in it.
(**Slide** of three greyhounds emerging as blurs caught floating in the air)

Dead Souls: Waft of the black air by the sides of the greyhound with its legs folded up on it is felt on the surface of one's skin.

Akira: It reemerges in the air roiling.

Just take away people's disability payments. And see what happens.

Defoe: The immensely tall slender limbs with the head centered on them barely moving walk toward the wrestling ring in it.

Akira: Linear can also be fake memory.

Defoe: It has to be linear to be still then. (**Slide** of greyhound)

Officer (he moves as if bouncing/touching a basketball): Sides of the flank with the legs move alongside the head on long limbs walking in the dark.

Dead Souls: The greyhound's legs are hanging in the air flying so that it's barely seen.

Akira: There's a visible roiling and it reemerges in the air by him. (**Slide** of greyhound)

Defoe: Roiling of the velvet air in which floats the form with no legs, it's reentering toward him.

Running in black air, it's invisible then.

Lights. **Akira and Defoe** are seated on bar stools placed in a line to one side of or alongside the center platform. It suggests an outside stand or a restaurant.

Officer: (He says gently, speaking to himself):

Born with wealth, the president's wife pretending civilization professes women not working are family values.

So they are to work out of necessity, and also humble themselves to curtail themselves inside as nothing, at the same time.

(**Akira** exits)

Scene 4

(**Dead Souls** is seated on platform; **Defoe** paces)

Defoe (as if questioning herself earnestly):

We have to have no dreams occurring. Be only conscious.

Dead Souls: The corpse doesn't arise from culture.

Defoe (Sincere, questioning, speaking to herself):

When they mention the jewel here, it's a jeer as such at itself, at it. So to be quiet inside, not jeering, is to be the infant lying on the leaf in the sea now.

It's a part of oneself that's left a jewel.

Dead Souls (sarcastic): I had a friend. When dying of AIDS, he couldn't speak, his parents walking in and out taking his things — "Oh, I could use this T-shirt"— says "N-oo."

Defoe (continuing her stream of thought, referring to the jewel): Occurrence, it's not their market ever.

Dead Souls: But that's merely the conditions of the sumo who's floating head.

Officer is lying curled on shelf in blue light. Lights go to darkness, then dim with illumination on **the Officer** and **Dead Souls** who is seated on her knees on the platform. She's placed black teeth in her mouth through which she speaks. A coil of brocade is wrapped on her shoulders and strewn behind and around her.

Dead Souls: *I'm* not struggling. The entire day opens at once that is the plate of the ocean — on which the jewel intestine is released in the rain. Standing in it. The jewel itself releases. It's addicted to the day then. A valve.

Defoe (as if getting an idea): It's eliminating on the plain.

Dead Souls (Her voice may become shrill and wild, as deadpan:) Our vice president baited anyone thinking, as the 'cultural elite'? Here the cultural elite are people who can read at all.

23

Defoe (calmly, to no one): Maybe if we *do* make the small movements, they're not reproduced. (She shrugs.)

Dead Souls (as if she is looking at this, as if having been diverted to another topic): The owls sail swooshing at the croking frogs picking them off the black air.

The owls sail through the black air eating the frogs.

Sailing they grasp the frogs on the invisible field. We can't see them.

Music: **Dead Souls** lipsynch sarcastic as if singing but speaks the words after appearing to sing. **Slide** of greyhound. Then slide in Japanese of the following passage, as if vertical panels of newspaper columns.

(flapping the brocade):

Government prods the people into cattle chutes where they are robbed by bankers and businessmen.

(Her tone relaxes) It's easiest to rob the public by working right at the bank.

Defoe: Seeing the image of sumo

Dead Souls: delicately imposed on him
he's carried even with the blue night
It continues, in compartments.

Defoe (getting defensive): So?

Dead Souls (shrugs): So we're just the market, what's that? It appears to be memory.

A play being short time resembles the physical state, lucid and has no other place.

Dreams should not occur at all, in the sleeping state.

Those while asleep can enter into one standing in ordinary activity, into the physical state.

Does one see cows from that?

(Lights dim. **Dead Souls** removes black teeth, sheds brocade. Lights up.)

(referring to and indicating **Defoe,** says to audience):

One is in the light as if against it utterly fragile in order to see it. One is thus fragile to be it. *I'm* not.

They're wearing yellow ribbons sobbing to themselves. Crowds on the street are seen. If one isn't there as them, they get very even to each other.

Defoe: The corpse who's one's companion, and is not dead yet, is carried by the sumo and is even with the blue night in the crowd.

Officer (who's been lying curled on shelf in blue light, getting down from shelf. He's referring to the scene he's about to be in): They don't even meet.

(**VO of woman #3** and **slide** of text:)

So memory is

separate from

oneself then.

Scene 5

(The **Muscular Dove enters** — who is standing light illuminating him)

Muscular Dove: The man with the bleached white hair and the black eyebrows, like a muscular dove's, walks where the ball is in the incredibly blue sky.

(**Slide** of ball in the sky)

 Officer (uncurling): He's utterly silent, as is it, because it doesn't have noise in it.

Robinson Crusoe spoke of Silent Life, not having anyone to speak to for twenty-five years on an island. As if there were Silent Life just not speaking outloud, to people. But this is during the plague; here is Silent Life in reverse as if backward with people.

Muscular Dove: The man ran in the crowd and biting some, his mouth is translucent layers.

His lips in layers, one saw him roaming but blood only appeared on people in the crowd.

The oval of the flesh of his lips became a rim. A man standing in the crowd, not near him, had this rim as of lips thinly in blood on him.

One had thick blood as in petals coming from a mark on her.

A woman dragged a cord behind her through the crowd where people ran.

Muscular Dove sings. **Slide** of text of the directions, which are: "All texts are written by hand in color drawings; in other words, prior to printing or the same as this printing."

(**Slide** of text of song. **Song**: referee calls and saxophone)

I seem to have been born one thing. That's the plate. Utterly silent is just in one's flesh.

Leaving there is the end.

(**Muscular Dove** exits)

Scene 6

Dead Souls: (explaining, in fully lighted set and room as if play is over): This is the serial.

The serial in the newspaper is the same as lip reading. Cause it appears to come from one source. Paintings are in the advertisements on the billboards: so this is vertical radical space because it is constructed, what floats in the air, such as people floating.

Similarly, the vision may be an ad for some product. For example, this could be an advertisement which is the form of beauty now.

A hyena is swimming amidst the lilies.

Distinguishing from floating in front of the lasso.

That barely comes up. The hyena gets the infant in its mouth and swims with it.

It's swimming between the lilies on the lake with it. That could be for something to drink. So as not to go back to it being a dream.

Scene 7

(Series of **slides** of sumo wrestlers begins, music of their referee calls and saxophone)

Akira: (in response to **Dead Souls**): Events take place, singly, at a rhythm that is their simple occurrence, seen. It isn't planned.

Defoe (to no one): A vast mass is floating on the plate of the ocean.

A sumo lies in the thin surf, floating on it.

The sumo swims, barely seen.

Dead Souls: We make that leaning on counters eating at restaurants out grind on being so that it *is* that and not visible.

(**Slides** of sumos fade)

Akira: One has a whiskey bottle in that building and that building where I go, where it's kept for me, so communicating with associates is fast and delicate.

Any that's consistent is our delusion.

(Akira addresses the Officer singing)
Dead Souls is the manager of the wrestling ring....(turning to Dead Souls, sings) Boss....

Dead Souls pouring beer for **Officer** and bowing, as if trying to draw his attention away from his duties. He refuses, indicating tea instead.

Defoe: I had an operation, as if close to ghouls. I woke up at 5:00 in the morning the second day seeing, from high in the hospital, the light begin and come into the sky over the whole city. I returned in that experience to being around the age of eighteen, what's only then, elated, excited from the day beginning, only. Many days being there endlessly without death ever. The word to say it is "hopefulness", a sensation which means nothing to one, and disappears, as an adult (a man got worried when I described this) as it is not realistic.

That elation existing on no extinguishing is realistic. I'm going to experiment with having that excitement — that the life is elating and endless.

Not knowing one's mortality.

What if being only excited, returning to that of an eighteen-year-old not a child, and having hopefulness without any death known or existing (seen) —

can't even be expressed if not ever existing — is *being* realistic?

It isn't. Just as such, what isn't mature. I was *there*. I'm going to experiment with being that.

Dead Souls: The vast silken gelatin has great force.
(**Slides** on front and side walls of sumo wrestlers. Music: saxophone and referee calls)

Defoe: Go up Santa Monica Boulevard or somewhere, a sumo getting out of the surging Mercedes and walking on traffic like water, really vast strolling on the sidewalk by the cars.

Officer: A cry goes up in silence of the ball floating in brown dust of the sky hanging in shacks and arcades with underneath the boys rising to reach it.

A **slide** is shown of a ball in space, amidst the continuous slides of sumos in fighting and squatting positions. Music: referee calls of sumo match, and saxophone.

Akira: One would think this is easy. It appears easy. It is.

Shadow-Akira seen standing at one side says in Japanese Defoe's next passage.

Defoe: Out strolling taking a breath from the car, they're in lanes shimmering on water.

Akira: That's the heat on them.

Dead Souls: The sumo vast floating in light is by the windows of shops in passing.
(She moves on the rope taut emanating from under her robe as if she is pulled swaying from back stage.)

Defoe: Sumo grasping the vast stock of the other has shot forward, already — whose motions are all slow.
Stagger grappling up on each other unmoving.
There's slow. The vast gelatin squatting.

Akira: The vast gelatin shot forward. When it wasn't seen.

Defoe: One time, they're huge jockeying around the ring gently.
The vast silken slabs barely move. Then flips him.

(Continue **slides** of sumos in many positions)

Akira: Barely moving, the sumos are both thrown from the ring on each other. Violence isn't being reproduced by simple actions.

Lights dim to darkness, then up to light on **Akira** on platform who moves on his knees as if he's wearing a kimono, though he's in a loose hip suit, and opening invisible sliding doors to look at the night. He moves like a Japanese woman, as if there are memories of someone else unknown to the one moving.

Akira: Sumos passing like immense birds on the roof of the building.

Defoe: (not visible, from the dark, exiting): They're strolling on the roof in the dark.

Akira: That's making a separation. We're elated to wake up. But held apart in the slack blackness, it occurs.
　　　If we repeat the origins of ordinary occurrences in the *way* they appear mysterious to us, it is *how* they occurred.

Scene 8

(**Defoe** enters speaking to herself)

Defoe: One doesn't see when it happened back in it when one is making exactly the motions of the market *now*.

>action solely
>is what's outside

Officer (sitting on shelf in blue light, with his legs hanging off the shelf so that he is above Dead Souls):

>It out there occurs first. And one's not born. Yet

is in it.

>In the morning, there's the huge light sky coming up.

>Memory's being involuntary and repeats things
that do not occur — we have to do that — so that its motions are the same as there. (She exits)

Scene 9

Darkness. Then a **slide** of a sumo wrestler squatting forward. It's projected above the platform on which **Dead Souls** stands. She may be coiled in a long strip of brocade. **Officer** is coiled like a bow on the shelf that's attached to the back and above the platform; as this scene continues, he's curled illuminated by a blue light so his blue uniform glows. At the beginning of the scene, a samurai enters (**Defoe** disguised, with something across her face) dressed in samurai armor (cardboard plates may be attached on helmet, and on the shoulders and waist, decorated with bands of army stripes). A leaf fan and Birds of Paradise are attached to the back and are seen behind the head. The samurai stands at the right of the platform. (Or samurai armor may simply hang on stage, with no person.) **Muscular Dove** comes in wearing long soft white wings and a mask of a blond man with black eyebrows. The **Muscular Dove** and the samurai stand on either side during this scene with **Dead Souls**, the illuminated curled **Officer** in the center.

Muscular Dove: Read the Muscular Dove's lips. Here reading is only that.

Not to do so is really frightening, not to be able to negotiate the place one is in.

Dead Souls: Coming to the top of that stairs, the unraveling of the folds of robes, she stands him having pulled the member out of her before.

The folds open where he'd put the member in but then pulling it out.

(**Dead Souls** may gently whip a rope emanating from under her robe and tied backstage so that it appears that both she and the sumo are swimming on it.)

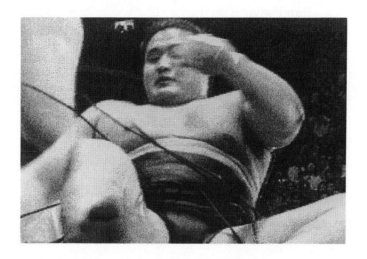

And with it open, him pulling it out.

(**Song**): The picture is given before the event occurs. It occurs as a given beforehand as if a fact.

So impression's delicately the same as it. For an instant.

(**Slide** of the text of her song is shown on the side wall)

Dead Souls (stands with her back to the audience. She's facing slide of sumo):

Sitting on him with it up in her comes, on him who's flat under her turning.

She's flat on him and turns, lying on him. He comes.

On each other flat coming, they're barely visible
to each other
Sumo swims on the rise of a wave, barely visible.

The sumo wrestler's eyes are tiny fish lost in the
mass that's floating head on it.
The woman's folded with her legs up on her.
He puts his member in her.

Hovering over her, he draws it out. It's night.

Putting it in, he hovers on her, with it in, with
her legs folded up on her. (**Slide** of greyhound)

Scene 10

Dead Souls (Series of **slides** of greyhounds, which
make a carryover from the greyhound shown after the
love scene):
Dead Souls had been in the dog racing stadium.
The dogs run so fast they're pins.
The figure scuttling over the stands, the stadium
is blasted in silence with the clouds shot, the greyhounds hanging under them.

36

(**Grey Silk Suit enters blowing in the wind.** His disguise is mask with stitched in, pressed mouth like a hole)

(**Slide** of the factory. Then **slide** of the ball in air.)

Scene 11

Slides of Grey Silk Suit running in gyration of the flying worm in a street of local city. **Grey Silk Suit** enters as if chasing someone. He moves uttering a groan of pain in a billow of wind in the following 'location' with several slides shown behind him of a factory pouring fumes into the sky in a tropical setting. Music: cicadas screaming.

Grey Silk Suit: The officer stops in the sun at a man staggering static in the street. There's no one around. Dogs run by them, as he's standing in the street.

> Outside the car.
>
> The glazed day is only light that are figures in it.
>
> That minute motion is so stilled it's not visible.

(**The Muscular Dove** comes in)

Muscular Dove: Out on the hot night boulevard, the lines of traffic are panting, stalled.

A person standing on the street appears, his lips thick petals, far from a man running. Then isolated, the unfolding petals have blood on them.

Far ahead of that person, a man screaming runs into the weak crowd to bite those still standing there, who don't have any mark on them.

(Blood comes from the lips of **Muscular Dove's** mask)

(**V.O. of woman as Grey Silk Suit** floats wildly in the wind): A man came into the street where I was standing in it, close to my childhood neighborhood, and was introduced to me by a friend standing there with me. The man began to remember 'me', from my last name, being an incredible runner. I said No, that was my sister Lynne, my little sister.

His son was beat by her. (He said only his son's name, implying the relation. My mother had said at the time that this man's daughter had had a nervous breakdown, as a kid, from their moving to an all-white block.) He beat everyone running. But not Lynnie, the man said in a melodious repetition, she could beat *all* the boys. I didn't know this. I have to dream, but I can't see them occur in waking life anywhere. (So fast, crouched she would sprint out in front of them.) Al could beat the boys; but not Lynnie, she could beat *all* the boys.

She was doing that, running — as she was younger — separate from me. That seemed incredible.

An entire lifetime had occurred, been spent, already.

A part of a good life is spent preparing to die. While aware of this, I was preparing to live, just that — only.

She's in time only in the physical state and separate from me. The physical state not being suppressed in itself, is not from any memory.

The physical state is only then; where she could beat *all* the boys.

'Preparing' to live, that's all that is, is only now, where there's nothing behind, or occurred.

That's why action is a project, which is to exist; is only in the physical state.

Her being a runner was *then*, not known to me. It is *to* happen. One is separate. She was seeing. Everyone is clear-sighted as their physical state, then.

(**Grey Silk Suit** ceases wild floating movements)

VO of Defoe: Passing the small open shops, there's the smell of fried potato cakes. Then Defoe is standing by the railroad crossing which has the arm down barring the tracks. It's evening but entirely light. Glancing down, she sees a huge cicada clinging on her clothes. Its lace wings with heavy veins in them are folded plastered on her. The screaming in waves can't be heard. Involuntarily, she lets out a scream seeing it.

(Music: cicadas. **Defoe** who has been turning slightly in the wind, from the fan, lets out a scream, slapping at her dress and face.)

Muscular Dove: A man seeing Jean Cocteau's *Orphée,* saying it frightened me tentatively yet inured says I'd never paid attention to content before. He sees behavior as convention everywhere except the physical wilderness.

There are no people: but that condition has to arise here *not from people.*

In this country, content is action solely.

I want to place comparisons together, in the same space, floating peacefully.

But they are as if pressed where they can't touch.

The corpse floating in the blue night, the *night* isn't dreamed.

Defoe: There are no ads on billboards there, at evening. So it's the same as it.

It can't be avant garde because it's beauty.

Reduce it to being business as that's our inner motions only. It's not outside. It doesn't exist there.

Officer enters: (as if giving an explanation of the Muscular Dove): Which the other man sees surprised.

to make the same motion

(The Muscular Dove stands lips moving. **Slide:** of the factory from a different vantage.)

Officer: Man emerges staggering in the sun ball on the street.

We think language at all is romantic, rather than that it's seeing.

For the Romantics, the actual ones, making the realistic to be incredible was just seeing the real.

Our society doesn't realize either it's being incredible or real. This is simple.

(**Slide** of a ball in the sky. Then different **slide** of the factory.)

The boys playing volleyball, who're almost slaves in factories foreign-owned by us, while our factories close, are only in the day. They're separate from the night being there: the night isn't dreamed.

Forming of unions is crushed.

(Real ball is thrown in from back stage) (**Slide read by V.O. of woman:**

I write under a pen name. He vomits the lotus field.

Goya)

(**Slide** of Balthus "La Toilette de Cathy" collaged with speech bubble of sail boats on blue emanating downward from male figure's mouth. Below is a caption which reads: He vomits the lotus field. Bubble from the naked Cathy standing is: as they do in memory.)

Muscular Dove: One is utterly silent in the blazing blue with the bulb opening. It's dragged on a rope by her.

One doesn't suffer. It unfolds from the tight fur, from no one.(He exits)

Defoe: Torn by jealousy, someone who was ill ran in a crowd biting because those standing were to be still living. He's roaming running aimlessly.

He's running in their stream. The moon's in the stream sailing.

Sailing, while a crowd in its lighted stream cries for infants to be forced to be born.

(naively): Living in misery, they have a volleyball teamhouse at the company where they can have showers at least. (**Officer** grimaces at her)

41

(**Officer** gets back on the shelf, lies on the shelf looking down on the two women and warmly chats with them by mime, while **Defoe** actually speaks.) (**Slide** of a ball)

Defoe (cavalier): I think trash is thought.

One's corpse companion who's not dead being carried by sumo so they're even with the blue night

is not dreamed.

It doesn't conceal the crowd crying. This place is the same as dreamed. Except it's not; they're not akin even.

(**Officer** exits)

(**Defoe** speaks 'simply', to the audience as if speaking with one person.)

A dream in the middle of the day was impinging trying to break through to be my conscious day activity; I was standing there with it trying to be in my present action. I couldn't really remember the dream, though it had been frightening. I'd had no awareness of it or when it first occurred.

My mind was collapsing to be one, at emergence.

I was having a 'psychotic' experience. One is seeing a shred clearly while being in a healthy state, they're in a blue dim floating.

I was in it, as it was in shreds, with it going on at the same time I'm standing being in an ordinary activity.

There's no sense that it arises from suppression of the physical state with cognition not really existing in it.

If cognition is entirely occurring in the state of a sort of suppression which illuminates a real sky horizon it isn't cognition producing the dream.

The dim blue burning softly occurs again, every day.

Dead Souls: Seeing the corpse with the rose-colored gel coiled in its center, the coil in it is luminous.

The corpse floats gently in the gel. It has striated muscles, cords of leather, a bird that runs.
(**Slide:** of leathery chest and back muscle diagram, which has shape of samurai armor.)

A business is a success if it's big.

VO of woman #3 (pronounces rather thunderously):

At first there was mimicry, but then there wasn't mimicry of anything. Not at all.

(The following is enacted while it is spoken. **Grey Silk Suit worm-face** flies to **Akira** clinging to him like a worm, flapping.)
Akira: The sumo in the ring wiping his hands of the ceremonial salt and swaying heavily to the side, a hippo I met on the path in the rushes with the dawn sky over us eyes cast down, who swerves thunderous into the rushes, the man is similarly early at dawn.

His intestine the jewel sack released, the woman Dead Souls is already without thought entering the ring to him. Akira entered, also at dawn, when this is seen as the mind.

Dead Souls: Action isn't the mind yet when brought to its occurrence it is.

Akira: Akira is stabbed by the faceless or knitted face at dawn in the rushes, when seen as the mind. Entering the ring Akira with the knifing figure plastered on him is a lung cavity in whose cells or cylinders is the blade. Yet at dawn he's carried in the street.

Action isn't the same as one, so it's dawn. Flesh recedes not born, there, but it's only in the other's seeing it. So him blue curled in the dark air is without mind.

(Limp, he exits, drawn savagely by **Grey Silk Suit** who has uttered cries of pain)

Dead Souls: The image is subjecting everything to occurrence. This only exists here overtly, clumsily. To subject in love with his flesh to occurrence.

Defoe: The hippo met on the path darting aside eyes turned to the side huge on the dawn can't get into being born the bullrushes are born at a time there. Subject to the dawn.

They silently 'reenact' an event we haven't seen, as if it is deja vu, **Dead Souls'** shooting of **Grey Silk Suit** who is about to slash **Defoe** in the past. **Dead Souls** holds the gun with her arms straight out police style. **Defoe** enters into the motion of the two at the last instant, when **Dead Souls** has raised the gun to shoot **Gray Silk Suit** Man: so they return to the 'original' sequence of motions. **Grey Silk Suit** is floating in the wind, which blows from the fan. He's making threatening motions with the knife, getting closer to **Defoe**; as she moves swirling in reference to his motions, but then speaks the following as if to herself internally:

Defoe: If we're not disrupted continually, that's related to death. We have to start our existence still. We haven't done it yet.

(**Grey Silk Suit** ceases that 'past' motion. They seem to emerge out of that past location. Exits)

Maybe memory itself is joy.

Act II: Scene 1

(**Slide** held during **voiceover**. Then **Defoe** is alone)

VO of Defoe: Have them in the army. It's a way of making a living.

Man pelted by magnolia blossoms that are flung by the Santa Ana wind. He's arising from the car, uncoiling.

---

fan as **Akira** enters and is pelted from back stage with magnolia blossoms.

Defoe: There are some people who like large stores, chains.

The magnolia blossoms hurl he's unfurling in them through that wind that's hot as when rolling down the car window at an instant of time in which it seemed to burn one's face.

That's closed together distilled.

People just came up to the trough and are seen running. In the surveillance beam, at night.

Akira: Sumo strolling on the hot night, up the street. Cars stall on the stream. A sumo getting out of a car in the stall vast strolls in the neon light.
(Music: cicadas)

VO of Officer: The restaurants are still open and the wind is a roar that may not be heard, when he has the blossoms stuck on him. A blue sky

VO of Dead Souls: if it could be seen

VO of Officer: is blown itself.
(**Slide** of blue blurred rim which hovers over actual **Officer** lying on top of shelf where his blue clothes are illuminated almost touching the drawn swatch of line.)

Dead Souls: They're stuck on him not moving as he's not moving flailing, his loose suit billowing.

Officer: Palm Springs is filled with wind.

Dead Souls: The valley, where the farmers had labored, on their knees as in their rice fields leaving their homes, is a sky of dirt flying so that the waves of heat rising quivering are in sheets of soil.

Officer: A woman losing her infant from her being over-worked in that intensely quivering sky became depressed and ignored the next infant when it came so that the other children carried it.

Defoe: Thin red line comes on the quivering fields, in the heat.

(Slide of red water-color line) **(Defoe and Akira** have gotten up onto the platform during the **VO)**

Officer (gently speaking as if of another event, and of some other): Not he who's the tufts of bear fur on the plates. Rather, the one with the plates quills of plates. Which peeled from him, the chest breathing softly, is lying in its own rose gel.

She holds the soft breathing chest of who'd put the member in. His eyes swim. He quivers.

It's interesting how you have to explain what you see, in order to convey it, more (so) than what you think (that is, how you view some issue.)
(Screaming cicadas) (Silent **slide:**)

that's not memory actually

so he's lonely in that he's dead
the actual rim's written itself.

Akira: (He reveals his chest plate of rosy gel and striated leather muscles — it's changed in appearance — pulling open a flap on his chest). A blossom or two is stuck to his body.

He comes in a blossom on him. At night it's so black and warm, not there, that the cicadas scream in waves, wave after wave rising carried in it so that just at dawn there's an instant of silence where one can't sleep

Defoe: but who wants to

Akira: and they begin in a wave that's the glazed day then.

Puts in the long stem

Defoe (She's sitting up on him. Says gently and seriously):

sitting on it. Comes, turning.

One could be that inside. Or *appear* to be that.

I'm doing these motions which if they coincide with standardized love make people jeer. Because it resembles love. They laugh.

(Asks insecurely) Is that what makes them jeer? Or that it's me, one?

(Then Akira lies on Defoe and fully clothed they make love realistically while Akira says the following:)

Akira: Man pelted by magnolia blossoms in the Santa Ana wind:

> bending over her, he puts his member in her.

> Then trembling on her takes his part out
> She puts his part in and flat comes
> takes the part out
> Him not having come then
> and putting it in her comes lying on her

Dead Souls (She may get up on the platform, and lie reclining in the brocade alongside the lovers as if in a nearby location, akin to horizontal scrolls of people in compartments in *The Tale of Genji*):

> Goya wrote this so the solely inner is reasoning. Not reasoning being first.

> Goya wrote this so one's solely inner is reasoning. The solely inner in one is second.

Akira (concentrating only on Defoe, but speaking of himself):

> Dark opal companion floating on the stream, the dog with no legs flies by him — so fast that the legs, folded on it, can't be seen.

After **Defoe** finishes the entire passage, up to "to each other", the following is repeated, sung. It is sung by a soprano and tenor and played by a saxophone. Can be sung by **Defoe** as **Akira** exits.

49

Defoe: Flat twisting, comes
　　　　Then he takes it out.

　　　　She's lying flat, and not touching her
　　　　with his part in her though
　　　　she comes.
　　　　He's lying flat on her coming
　　　　so that they are barely visible
　　　　It's night
　　　　to each other

Dead Souls (she may say this while the song is beginning 6th line): Positions of erotica occur in this which
are love then. In those exact minute motions; these have
a rhythm of presentation in this that occurs in spurts
and not planned. When it is subject to only its movement, it has no other reflection. It isn't social perception;
or rather, is it *only* then. What's that?

　　　　The illusion is cultivated that events have already occurred and the response people have and have
had to these. It isn't arising there.

(Silent **slide**)

　　　　There's no center
　　　　so we occur first

(**Muscular Dove** enters)

Muscular Dove: Since there's nothing happening here
that'll be the only action.

　　　　Conformity is not a relation to *one*. So have one
squeezed to be bobbing up then on the red sheet

　　　　The ball's a red sheet swimming.

The sumo on the wave is narrowed to the rim of the ball's dilation.

He's in the dilation with no effort.

(**Slide** of greyhounds in blur of motion as if turning on each other in air)

Scene 2

Darkness. Then **slide** of greyhounds on center wall. **Officer** is curled on his back on the shelf as if in the sky.Defoe and **Dead Souls** walk.

(Silent **slides:**)

　　written's on space

　　---

　　floats on its rim

Dead Souls: A businessman is beating a figure in a black robe.

Defoe: So we have to efface ourselves more and more, and be naive so there's no movement, in order to see that very thing oneself is expressing.

Officer: So there's no childhood.

　　A figure in black robes down beaten the jewel intestine glimmers. We have to see each part, or component with them isolated in it.

　　The structure is forgotten as a whole.

　　In this, what one hears is forgotten though the structure still continues.

　　One forgets the structure, never sees it. Seen in the center as if a coal, when the figure is beaten, the jewel intestine is there.

Defoe: The criteria of the small shop appears in order not to reflect one.

If it were reflecting one, we couldn't start one's existence.

I can't stay in one place, or have the same job.

Then I can be happy.

The beaten black robes drags a cord behind it. It drags this long cord which is attached under the robe.

Figures being beaten are everywhere around it.

(**Slides** of greyhounds begin.)
Dead Souls: The bulb in one while lying on the lotus field begins to open, inside one.

Officer: The greyhounds are pins floating in the air.

Defoe: appearing to move on one's retina

Officer:: It didn't begin. The air's clear.

Dead Souls: They're racing their legs folded up on them hanging

Officer: and then reemerging on this track.

Defoe: They're out before seeing.

Officer (sarcastic, addresses **Defoe** and **Dead Souls**):
    Gentlemen.... (They start, or jump)

Defoe (becoming feverish): Gentlemen are empty hacks. They just don't know it. That's what that *is*. They regard actions as lower. So they imitate not being that. It's backwards.

Officer: *Then.*

Defoe: They don't know that. Not imitating one's own motions is joy.

(reads **slide**):

Not being a heroine: which is really being one then, by commenting on their really being heros from their *not* being heros now — from their not having that illusion. They're avant garde, though a heroine is not. That is modern form — in newspaper font. They think.

It isn't nothing yet.

(naively considering:) That's thinking that perception is inherently inaccurate.

Dead Souls: It is.

Voiceover of woman #3: The trotting hyena comes up and beds Dead Souls.

It's going by in its cavalcade on the road.

The thrashing muzzle of the president gets out of the car.

Then it's trotting back with its humped neck swiveling on its haunches.

It trots back to the car afterward.

(They're all suspended. **Dead Souls** then steps forward, speaking to herself seriously, quietly.)

Dead Souls: Thrashing, I was in the mud, lotuses growing everywhere around me.

There was one in me, a bulb in fur squeezed out of me. It was on a long rope.

The bulb's huge petals opening in me, I was crying. Lying in the mud with it pressing me and then it's translucent lying on the mud behind me.

I looked at it.

I ran dragging the bulb in fur with it attached at the rope.

On the street with the cord touching the street, the bulb is dragged in the crowd. One time.

The crowd parting with my rope dragging in it, one man cradles the bulb with its sack in translucent layers. The pressed skin made an opening where it had broken off having been attached at the rope.

Defoe (sympathetically, quietly to **Dead Souls**): I don't think you have to change to compromise *anything*.

Akira: (wandering through) It's linear reappearing washing as the only conformity.

He who's of the people starving, and fought his own looting soldiers who's himself hungry. I'd been in the LAPD. This is reemerging, linear, and so it's silent.

Memory is behind, so that's not the only way to learn.

Here they think not ever knowing death is being corralled and safe in life.

What did they think was going to happen? It's the same as the order of what you do, ordinarily.

Defoe staring at him: The plates of feathers sockets of quills fighting the soldiers who're themselves starving it's like being sent on a suicide mission, in the inner self. Yet the quiet imageless eyes float downward.

Dead Souls: Limbs curl like a bow in the dark.

Defoe: If one's alone, there's roiling of the coagulated dark hanging, and reemerging calm.

Scene 3

Defoe: His eyes lowered float in their sockets.
(**Slide of Akira's** eyes, swimming downcast)

      Business is a success. Who's somehow but floating. Inaccessible to me. The quills on the plates, with the plates on me. They were cold. His eyes in their sockets looking down gently float on me there.

Towards the end of her speaking a **slide** comes on of a young samurai seated with his eyes gazing downward. Then the following while the slide is still there.

Akira: Business is the rim. It floats, washes on it. So it's on itself visible. It rests in the stream of people thrashing giv ing birth. Then infants emerge.
      To catch oneself trying or wanting to change events is one.

Dead Souls: That's pleasure in the city, for the new person.

> Sumo sagging on the thin surf floating carcass
> with the red rim is head on it.
> bulb on wave
> that's thin

Defoe: Peddling on the bicycle on the surf in the sun
> and the sumo is floating in it.

Shadow-Akira seen at side says in Japanese Dead Souls' next passage before she says it.

Dead Souls: Have no memories. These are tracing someone else's. The quills on the plates of the eye sockets float alongside.

> People running are aimless then in a crowd.

Defoe: One induces movement that is minute and has no function

Akira: requires complete attentiveness.

Dead Souls (disgusted): Everyone has to pretend to be goody-two-shoes here. It's backward.

Defoe (explaining sweetly): It's a form. There aren't our characteristics. At all. In the place.

> Then this itself is mimicked. Where it's not itself. Then we're backward.

Akira (lipsynch song in a serious manner of tenor. As he begins, a tape of screaming as if he is a movie idol is heard for an instant):

Akira is to find the child. There isn't going to be that again.

So there's no separation between them.

(**Akira** stops lipsynch)

VO sings: We watch someone beaten rolling on the video. Then the jury says he was in control, when he's being beaten there.

Dead Souls: One's companion is even with one
who's a corpse not dead yet carried
in the blue night in the crowd.
Sumo is head on green wave
in the blue night
seen on the eyes floating

Defoe: (Sung) The companion corpse not dead yet who's carried
so that he's even with the blue night
is similar in it.

It's just what everyone sees, or it can't *be*.

A fur bulb of peaceful fetus or cocoon hanging on a string from the ceiling which was behind the cloud is dropped by **Dead Souls** and floats on the string. A slide of a creature in a Bosch painting is shown on the center background.

Dead Souls: If he's on the green wave floating one can't tell if he's riding or the night is on the green wave. It's curled on it. This is the utmost scrutiny.

Defoe (lies down, speaking from sleep): It's the eyeless deaf figure hanging twisting in the pan of the sky as if it were a coagulation in which it's caught.

We send troops in to feed them.

Officer speaks as if calling the song from offstage. **VO** of sings.

Song:

The eyeless lidless beating, the immense shining plate is thin and doesn't hold it. It beats in it anyway. It's the child.

Song:

The white eyeless thrashing is in this basin that's everywhere.

Officer (calling from offstage as if singing as echo of referee calls):

Where the red ball of the sun would spread out bouncing on the rim sometimes, under which it then disappears, the eyeless thrashing is floating as if looking in.

Defoe: Linear really has to be carried on until it's still.

Dead Souls: Finding out where one has violated something by putting material in where it won't go.

Akira (to himself): One doesn't know when it happened.

What occurs isn't a condition of sense. Isn't first.

Nor is the other — sense, not just given to it — first. It's removed as a condition of anything.

One has to start one's existence.

Then I can be happy.

Don't imitate my own movements, in myself — at the same time they're occurring.

Murmuring waking just at that moment so it's eliminated, I have a dream of my own older sister swimming down as if in an aquarium to get her dress for her own funeral, that's in the green space above and not visible. Held before me floating behind as if on it and my being curled frozen. The space in which I was frozen, curled, was the same as that in which she was swimming, though I am outside it. I know I won't ever speak with her again in our long life that's ahead because she doesn't want to.

That's just any dream, what I had now.

I'm not seeing myself. Yet that's still occurring.

Defoe (to herself as if to remind herself): See matter that is just at not dreamed. At all.

Akira: Held curled is the setting clasping his rose-colored gel coil.

That's conscious matter which I make up.

A silent dream would require being quiet inside.

VO of Officer: The light thin morning holds the rosecolored gelatin that is coiled with him clasping it.

Dropping, in the moment of something occurring, *then*, it's there still, flapping.

(fur bulb is pulled back up behind cloud by **Defoe**)

Akira: I have to hold this to be absolutely realistic. I don't know what *it* is.

I dreamed of a hyena that was on burning lily fields. It was swimming ahead.

This dream is the same as an ad or a billboard and so it's eliminated.

I swim in it free now. It could be for something to drink.

Scene 4

Grey Silk Suit enters (he moves very slowly in wind appearing to walk with **Akira**)

V.O. sings (repeat five times to saxophone music): The man seen on the video being beaten rolling as they club him, the jury says he was in control. But he is in the crowd.

Grey Silk Suit: (Said as if confidentially to **Akira** as they float there)

We can't keep up with being resembled.

Figures in the mud come up. These are so addicted, even children, they suck gasoline in tubes. Almost lying silent in the crowd, while they sip in clusters, some wander forward. They have to have it.

Someone else, not they, ran in the crowd where they're sipping on tubes, and biting running aimlessly crossing his own path, he's then stopped by us shooting him many times. They just keep coming, holes opening in him amidst them.

(Silent **slide:**)

The rim creates the newspaper

Akira: So we can't see the movement that's come from them if we're seeing it as reflecting.

If we're not seeing it as reflecting it's not that movement either. Being in it, our culture can't see itself, by saying that's oneself.

I don't dream the dogs.

Grey Silk Suit: Our actions are the same as what occurs realistically.

We don't narrow to and on its (actions) rim which is just one's thinking anyway. It doesn't have a rim.

It doesn't exist. So an action, not ever in relation to existence anyway, is only a setting. Bathos is in it.

Occurrence is isolated and freed from oneself.

(**Defoe** and **Dead Souls** are illuminated on or near the platform, chatting.

Dead Souls (to **Defoe**): They defend their mother, so that she'll go on saying how wonderful they are. Then they won't have to develop themselves. That's not love. It's self-serving.

Akira (to himself as contemplative aside):
     The action's only occurring alongside the line (of sky), the actual horizon.

Dead Souls: Rotting dog ballooning floating so that it's on the blazing blue.

(**Slide** of text, read by **Grey Silk Suit**):
     This screen is what occurs. Akira will have to consent to run drugs for the CIA, though he's in the LAPD, or they kill him. As their insurance, they will have Defoe run some from Bogota. She doesn't know that he's dead.

Dead Souls: Every paragraph — sometimes a line is a paragraph — is by itself. As if the segments are an expanse, or settings of separate compartments. Which don't blur into each other.
     The time in early adolescence when one is in (what other's would say) 'extreme' conflict later unfolds. Every night and day is separate. They may be serene in seeing the early components of that same conflict.

Defoe: When I had the operation recently, after, waking elated, I was free of even that conflict, of any; I could just be excited merely at any day beginning. For a moment, the multiple span was endless (which doesn't mean anything to the adult, as not being realistic). I will get back to this and do it.

Dead Souls: As long as it's linear, it's silent.

We want to be where we are really, but we can't.

If we 'aren't to have' a sense of ordering, which implies a basis, of oneself or 'government', which 'orders' — even the thought 'aren't to have' 'order' is an ordering in itself — (so the experience of *not ordering* doesn't even exist) — there's one's excitement at the beginning of days only.

(to no one:) It's not rebellion that's needed. At adolescence in 'extreme' conflict one is just *out there*, then.

(chatting with **Defoe**): It's the man jetting moving on the dark. That comes first.

Sacks, the infants after birth, begin dreaming, their eyes and feet twitching while they're asleep and dreaming. Since they have almost no age, what could they be dreaming? — of what was before birth, or what's *now* in them?

Defoe: This will never be seen again. (**Defoe** lies down on the platform to go to sleep.)

Dead Souls: Defoe dreams when she's just going into sleep so the picture occurs right before her.

(slide:)

written's | space
              |
          can't reflect
     crossing horizontally

in the newspaper

That's not memory actually

Scene 5

Defoe: In that, if the market is memory — still — actions have no memory. They're without a trace. Not 'themselves.'

Akira: Action movies here are a format. They have a certain time. That is success for people.

An hour and a half. This (that's minute movements) is a format, that's an action flick in another form.

The flesh has a certain time; that's its realm that's temporal. It makes that sense. The intellect can know transience but the body can't.

So have one's body know after. That's this form.

We make small movements that don't mimic anything except the form.

(Silent **slide** in handwriting:)
my teacher said my handwriting
was the worst he'd seen and here is this.

The following occur as if exactly at the same instant.
Defoe releases the bulb covered with fur which twirls.

Slide of rotting coyote landscape. **Dead Souls** responds with expression of grief.

Defoe: When it is at the inside of itself — not in *one*, (that doesn't matter) — then it's at its original motion, rather than being a dream.

    This is to make it not be dreamed.

    That's together distilled. A woman seen out thrashing on the ground.

    They say that's how events occur. The space collapses and *is* one.

(Silent **slide:**)

      written is in | columns that
      are across | that space.
                |

(**Akira** exits, **Officer** enters running)

Defoe: See the former president as a hyena swimming.

Officer: Now running wet on the bank with the helicopter pressed on me.

    I was running, the helicopter hanging following me. A rose hangs in it that's the sun. The ball hangs and dips.

    People rounded up and put in boxcars are like cattle. The sky can't open any wider then. There's no relation of it to them, so they don't have customs.

    They work without life. We do.

Scene 6

Dead Souls: The now former president's wife is a vicious hyena thrashing. Disemboweling. That's illuminated on the plate. It's moved slightly.

(Referring to and indicating **Defoe**): She rides a bicycle as a messenger, for a job.

This is supposed to be in the newspaper. To be printed in the newspaper as a serial as if it were Dickens' novels. Everyone reads them.

And the form of this is that way. In installments.

Don't have any other reference than serials.

Defoe (looking out): It makes no action moving as well. The greyhound's floating on the ocean.

It's head and back a pin with no legs.

Dead Souls: Sumo who with the black wave rolling on him floats on the rim of the green waves then, infants don't need to be born.

The crowd screaming hatefully that infants should be forced to be born, who wouldn't be here otherwise, they are given a physical state.

Defoe: The physical state is endless.

Dead Souls: We can just see their own simple occurrence, if that.

Defoe: Just keep going.

I haven't been sleep deprived.

The outside occurrence which is illusion but real comes from actually being in the ordinary activity, while not dreaming.

The 'illusion' (but it's real), which is outside not a function of memory, emerges, leaks into, standing being in ordinary activity.

Dead Souls (in a pool of light on the platform, speaks to audience): Frequently, one does nothing continually.

Sometimes, there's simply no need to doing anything. It is floating on it as it just is there.

(**Grey Silk Suit** in worm-mask, his suit billowing in wind — passes in dimmed light to **Dead Souls'** bed, clings to her and slashes her, murdering her)

Scene 7

(**Slide:**)
    So memory is
    separate from
    oneself then.

(Sumo referee calls begin)
VO of Defoe with background of referee calls:

The immense haunches of the sumo throws the other out of the ring.

They don't move. Are flattened up against each other on the vast stocks, which circle.

Then slaps him, and runs him forward, tossed out of the ring.

Shoppers go by. From a sound outside.

(referee calls fades)

V.O. of Akira: If we make this so simple it will not be what's public. Which is *its* joy.

It's flattened to be itself, which can't exist in the place.

I want to make sure that musical comedy doesn't come back.

That's us. So I'm to have no motive.

It's silent. I go to that building and that building where they have whiskey bottles for me. There's no development.

Akira: My contribution is that there are no images, at all, as they emerge.

(**Slides** of sumos. Sumo referee calls accompanied by saxophone composition.)

(**Akira** standing in audience): Streams of them on the crowd. Streaming on it. The streams, crowds strolling, shopping, are barely noticed.

The long cord coming from one is in the crowd.

The helicopter sinking and flying in the pea air so that the heavy pan rises which is only submerged reflecting a beam on the running figures

the beam follows a running woman who illuminated has the heavy extended belly.

An emerging bulb is seen in the half-light of the heavy pan that wallows and hangs browsing over it in the dense air.

I want this to have no images, as these occur only in action. That's at birth itself.

I'm not sleeping or actively dreaming though what occurs is illumined. It doesn't come from sleep.

Where there's an actual dream that attempts to leak through into present activity where one is standing, not knowing even that one had dreamed

or being able to remember what it is as it tries to occur

Defoe: it's the actions of the day united with the moon bulb swimming on the crowd in the stream.

Akira: That *can't* be remembered. So the two comparisons seen only to be held together, and paired there united peacefully, where one is alone.

Officer (revealed standing in audience): The bulb being born, it emerges on the ground subject to its own shape.

That's not originally so there's no angelic narrative.

It's narrative solely that's so simple there isn't any life.

(**Slide** of sumo, one in which he's fallen)

Sumo swimming to her on the black waves is gently coming for her.

The red rim on the neck she still moves wad-
dling kneeling. She moves on the knees.

(Light up of **Dead Souls** moving on her knees in kimono, a red line on her neck, in the background)

The corpse who's one's companion in the blue
night that isn't dead.

The night isn't, and doesn't have any life in it.

Akira: The emerging of the bulb from the thrashing
woman is stilled and occurring.

The suppressed physical is brought to where
there's no mind occurring — there's no image in the
blue night.

There can't be images, while occurring in the
blue night.

Where the suppressed physical state, while
being completely empty, carried as if in the bow of the
night where there's a horizon a line on which the man
floats, but doesn't come on that line — floats in front of
it on the rose horizon line, half in black a corpse so his
memory's not cognating this, it's been reduced to not
coming from outside.

(**Slide** of rose line above text: "rose horizon line, half in
black a corpse so his memory's not cognating this.")

Nothing comes from the outside here. The suppressed physical state goes on. Usually we can't see anything from that.

V.O. of woman: He was worn out wounded and he simply died while trying to stay in life.

It's *La Vita Nuova.*

Defoe (looks up): A stilled fly, on the blackness. The 'extreme' conflict in adolescence, which later may unfold as the serene observation in the adult.

Officer: When you're just going about ordinary activity it's unknown. So you can put any material in, where it doesn't belong.

Or where it's 'apparent'. It's the same as the order of what you do. The 'apparent' relation of events doesn't matter in it.

That's an experiment to see what's occurring.

Defoe: Jetting in the night ejaculating a black cloud on it, on which he hangs and jets, on the dense stream, the man coming to one on the night is that unknown, being.

Fear's nothing. Literally, we don't know *what* it is.

As he jets up to one through the darkness that's existing.

(**Defoe** picks up and begins carrying suitcase. Stands in the audience, in the semi-darkness)

Officer: She's voided it on the plate. Dropping the cocaine in the rain. Where the boys come up sucking gasoline.

Defoe: They come up sipping (really sniffing) it to be high.

She's out and it begins to rain, already in the pour, then coming up to her.

Voided it on the plate so that she's carrying nothing events occur solely.

(**Slide** of young samurai)

Akira: One doesn't know anything in the past. I'm completely unprepared.

(She's glances down at the suitcase she's carrying.)

Defoe: (Speaking to the audience): This was supposed to be in the newspaper. In installments.

Boys come up to those who are hardly alive. This is supposed to be just in the newspaper. From written panels that go on. That's pleasure. That's all. Don't have other form.

(Says rather insecurely): Is this clear?

The brazen herd coming at the trough to be mild. (There's loud heckling from a person in the audience. He 'boos' her savagely. She appears shaken but continues.)

Boys coming up to the plain, on which they sniff gasoline. Inhale the thin air. (She inhales.) They've been neutralized there at the trough and are meek calling. Not by it, *before*.

Then, they don't have their characteristics at all.

We're meek — in light — at the trough. That's our view itself.

That's linear so that it's still and silent.

Where were we going to begin our existence? (Referee calls begin and continue to the end)

Seeing occurs from using on it what doesn't
have that capacity in it

        as solely public

Akira: The man jetting on the stream of the night ejacu-
lates a black cloud. He flows back and forth by one.

      If this is action solely it is still not in one's sup-
pressed physical state.

      It is not even in one's physical state.

      It would get to be luminous stuff, by not being
even in or of oneself.

Slide: a blue and a rose red line, the lines joined but sep-
arating.

Defoe (looks at Akira): The non-existence of or no ordering by government and his jetting on the dark then ejaculating on the dark cloud in the night on which he
hangs, the proximity of these two *are* the vertical and
horizontal rim we're seeing.

      (tenderly:) This enables his existence in my scru-
tiny.

Officer (standing somewhere in audience): The beginning of the action has nothing in it.

The Heckler (comes forward clutching his back, as if
mocking someone else's complaining):

      On a walk, the cage of my back clamped over in
the pale blue, in its own steel pressed closed.

It can't open, the back pressed on its own self. Clamped, convulsed. Were the back to lie flat, face down, the Cedar Wax Wings would light on it.

Officer: Being inert not moving, out, when walking depressed — suppressed and when there isn't dreaming — is then close to or comprehends the man being clubbed rolling — and is where those recipients are not causing it.

Defoe: Blindly white gazing, so that the recipient of it isn't existing inside — and is still, fighting. Not seeing is flagelating inside — actual real moon sliver as memory only when it's being seen

> One can't not dream
>
> which isn't seeing. There isn't *other* in it
>
> dreaming not having memory either

(Referee calls with music continue softly, then rise.)

Officer: The bulb opens on it, on the long cord that's back in the crowd. It opens in huge petals, that aren't existing, in not being memory or the present, but in blooming is not oneself.

Having the vision of this is always oneself. This is only inner. So this *occurs* only, is outside attached on the cord that's dragging in the crowd.

(They are all standing in the audience, with behind them on the center back wall a vacant pure blue. Then darkness.)

Potes & Poets Press, Inc.
181 Edgemont Avenue
Elmwood, CT 06110

POTES AND POETS PRESS PUBLICATIONS

Mickal And, Book 7, *Samsara Congeries*
Bruce Andrews, *Excommunicate*
Bruce Andrews, *Executive Summary*
Bruce Andrews, from *Shut Up*
Rae Armantrout, from *Made to Seem*
Todd Baron, *dark as a hat*
Dennis Barone, *The World / The Possibility*
Dennis Barone, *Forms / Froms*
Dennis Barone, *The Book of Discoveries*
Lee Bartlett, *Red Scare*
Beau Beausoleil, *in case / this way two things fall*
Martine Bellen, *Places People Dare Not Enter*
Steve Benson, *Reverse Order*
Steve Benson, *Two Works Based on Performance*
Brita Bergland, *form is bidden*
Charles Bernstein, *Amblyopia*
Charles Bernstein, *Conversation with Henry Hills*
Julia Blumenreich, *Parallelism*
Paul Buck, *No Title*
John Byrum, *Cells*
O. Cadiot / C. Bernstein, *Red, Green & Black*
Abigail Child, *A Motive for Mayhem*
A. Clarke / R. Sheppard, eds., *Floating Capital*
Norman Cole, *Metamorphopsia*
Clark Coolidge, *The Symphony*
Cid Corman, *Essay on Poetry*
Cid Corman, *Root Song*
Beverly Dahlen, *A Reading (11-17)*
Tina Darragh, *a(gain)2st the odds*
Tina Darragh, *Exposed Faces*
Alan Davies, *a an av es*
Alan Davies, *Mnemonotechnics*
Alan Davies, *Riot Now*
Jean Day, *The I and the You*
Jean Day, from *No Springs Trail*
Ray DiPalma, *The Jukebox of Memnon*
Ray DiPalma, *New Poems*
Ray DiPalma, *14 Poems from Metropolitan Corridor*
Rachel Blau DuPlessis, *Drafts #8 and #9*
Rachel Blau DuPlessis, *Drafts 3-14*
Rachel Blau DuPlessis, *Tabula Rosa*
Johanna Drucker, from *Bookscape*
Theodore Enslin, *Case Book*
Theodore Enslin, *Meditations on Varied Grounds*
Theodore Enslin, *September's Bonfire*
Elaine Equi, from *Decoy*
Norman Fischer, from *Success*
Norman Fischer, *The Devices*
Steven Forth, *Calls This*
Kathleen Fraser, *Giotto : Arena*
Peter Ganick, *Met Honest Stanzas*
Peter Ganick, *Rectangular Morning Poem*
Peter Ganick, *Two Space Six*
Susan Gevirtz, *Korean and Milkhouse*
Robert Grenier, *What I Believe*
Jessica Grim, *It / Ohio*
Carla Harryman, *Vice*
Carla Harryman, *The Words*
Susan Howe, *Federalist 10*
Janet Hunter, *in the absence of alphabets*

P. Inman, *backbite*
P. Inman, *Think of One*
P. Inman, *waver*
Andrew Levy, *Reading Places, Reading Times*
Andrew Levy, from *salvage device plants*
Steve MacCaffery, from *Theory of Sediment*
Jackson Mac Low, *Prose & Verse from the Early 80's*
Jackson Mac Low, *Twenties (8-25)*
Barbara Moraff, *Learning to Move*
Laura Moriarty, *the goddess*
Sheila E. Murphy, *Literal Ponds*
Melanie Neilson, *Civil Noir*
Janette Orr, *The Balcony of Escape*
Jena Osman, *Ellerby's Observatory*
Gil Ott, *Public Domain*
Maureen Owen, *Imaginary Income*
Maureen Owen, *Untapped Maps*
Rochelle Owens, from *Luca*
Bob Perelman, *Two Poems*
Larry Price, *Work in Progress*
Keith Rahmings, *Printouts*
Dan Raphael, *The Matter What Is*
Dan Raphael, *Oops Gotta Go*
Dan Raphael, *Zone du Jour*
Stephen Ratcliffe, *Sonnets*
Stephen Ratcliffe, *spaces in the light said to be
    where one/ comes from*
Joan Retallack, *Western Civ Cont'd*
Maria Richard, *Secondary Image / Whisper Omega*
Susan Roberts, *cherries in the afternoon*
Susan Roberts, *dab / a calling in*
Kit Robinson, *The Champagne of Concrete*
Kit Robinson, *Up early*
Leslie Scalapino, *clarinet part I heard*
Leslie Scalapino, *How Phenomena Appear to Unfold*
Laurie Schneider, *Pieces of Two*
Spencer Selby, *Accident Potential*
Spencer Selby, *House of Before*
Gail Sher, *w/*
James Sherry, *Lazy Sonnets*
Ron Silliman, *B A R T*
Ron Silliman, *Lit*
Ron Silliman, from *Paradise*
Ron Silliman, *Toner*
Margy Sloan, from *On Method*
Pete Spence, *Almanak*
Pete Spence, *Elaborate at the Outline*
Thomas Taylor, *The One, The Same, and The Other, 7-9*
Diane Ward, *Being Another / Locating in the World*
Diane Ward, *Crossing*
Craig Watson, *The Asks*
Barret Watten, from *Two Recent Works*
Hannah Weiner, *Nijole's House*